Liberty Is Obedience To The Law

Eliphas Levi

Kessinger Publishing's Rare Reprints

Thousands of Scarce and Hard-to-Find Books on These and other Subjects!

- Americana
- Ancient Mysteries
- Animals
- Anthropology
- Architecture
- Arts
- Astrology
- Bibliographies
- Biographies & Memoirs
- Body, Mind & Spirit
- Business & Investing
- Children & Young Adult
- Collectibles
- Comparative Religions
- Crafts & Hobbies
- Earth Sciences
- Education
- Ephemera
- Fiction
- Folklore
- Geography
- Health & Diet
- History
- Hobbies & Leisure
- Humor
- Illustrated Books
- Language & Culture
- Law
- Life Sciences
- Literature
- Medicine & Pharmacy
- Metaphysical
- Music
- Mystery & Crime
- Mythology
- Natural History
- Outdoor & Nature
- Philosophy
- Poetry
- Political Science
- Science
- Psychiatry & Psychology
- Reference
- Religion & Spiritualism
- Rhetoric
- Sacred Books
- Science Fiction
- Science & Technology
- Self-Help
- Social Sciences
- Symbolism
- Theatre & Drama
- Theology
- Travel & Explorations
- War & Military
- Women
- Yoga
- *Plus Much More!*

**We kindly invite you to view our catalog list at:
http://www.kessinger.net**

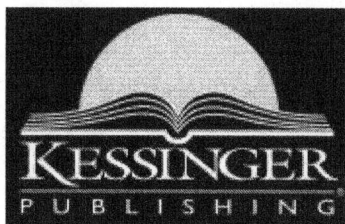

b15148386

Bible of the hierophants *is the Bible of liberty*. To believe without knowing is weakness; *to believe, because one knows, is power*.

———

Paradox II.—LIBERTY IS OBEDIENCE TO THE LAW

WHERE there is the spirit of God there is Liberty, say the Holy Scriptures.

Ye shall know the truth, and the truth shall make you free, said Jesus Christ. We should escape from the bondage of the letter to the liberty of the spirit, said the great Apostle.[1] Also he says, you have been

---

[1] The Deity is semi-male (? Hermaphrodite.—*Trans.*) in the Hebrew philosophy. The body of man is the vehicle of the three pairs of spouses, viz., the 2nd and 3rd, the 4th and 5th, and the 6th and 7th principles.

Irenæus speaks of " Bathos and Sige, Mind and Aletheia," each of them male and female. The three *pairs* of principles are then treated as three only, and we have the Trinity. The Jewish Kabala gives Macroprosopus his spouse, and the Microprosopus his *uxor*. (Liber Mysteri, I, 35, 38.)

" The anointed they call, male—female," says Cyril of Jerusalem, VI, xi. The SUN has the Pneuma for his spouse.

When Eliphas Levi speaks of Christ and his church, he means the Monad and its vehicle, the 7th and 6th principles. The Egyptian older Hermetic books give the first Quaternation, Monotes (Proarche, Proanennoetos, Mysterious and not to be named says

bought for a great price, do not any more make yourselves slaves of men. We are the children and not the slaves of God. We are the brothers and not the slaves of Jesus Christ.

The law was made for man and not man for the law, said again, the Divine Master. Liberty is the goal of man's existence; it is in this alone that his right and his duty can be reconciled; in this consists his personality and autonomy, and this alone can render him capable and worthy of Immortality.

Irenæus) and Henotes, the power that exists in union with "the Lord Ferho, the unknown, formless, unconscious Life" of the Codex Nazaræus.

This Monotes and Henotes, being the ONE, *sent forth*, not produced, but unconsciously emanated, a BEGINNING, as they call it (*arche*), before all things Intelligible, Unborn and Invisible, which *arche* is the MONAD (from the ONE).

In the West the religious philosophy of the Magi was first made famous under the name of Oriental Wisdom. Simon Magus teaches the doctrine of the Father, Son and Holy Spirit (*female*), and says that this Trinity had appeared amongst the Jews as Son, amongst the Samaritans as Father, and to other nations as the Holy Spirit. The Christian Trinity was bodily taken from the Kabalistic Nazarenes, who existed ages before the Western Christ, and to whom Jeshu (the Jesus of Lud, 130 B.C.?) belonged during the period of Alexander Jannæus (*a*).

"Life has built the house (body) in which you now stay, and the seven planets who dwell in it shall not ascend all into the land of Light.—" *Codex Naz.*, II, 35.

To free ourselves from the slavery of the Passions, from the tyranny of Prejudices, from the errors of Ignorance, the pains of Fear, and the anxieties of Desire, this is the Work of Life.

It is a question of being or not being. The free man is alone a man; slaves are but animals or children.

St. Augustine sums up the whole law in this fine saying: " Love, and do what you like." [1]

The free man can wish nothing but what is good, for all wicked men are slaves.

Following the spirit of our (*Catholic*) symbols, the freedom of man is God's great work; for this he permits a Hell to be hollowed out, and the hideous shadow of the Demon to be raised even to Heaven. It is for this that to the more than regal quietude of Divinity he prefers the sufferings of the accursed Humanity. God aspires to the cross of the malefactor

---

" Yes! the Chaldeans call the God. IAO, SABAOTH, he who is over the SEVEN Orbits (circles)—the Demiurge."—*Lydus de Mens*, IV, 38, 74. The seven orbits are the seven principles, the three couples with the house of flesh.

" Beam of the sun that hath shone the fairest light of all before the *Seven*-gated Thebes, thou hast at length gleamed forth, O eye of golden Day."—Sophocles, *Antigone.*—E. O.

(*a*) Alexander Jannæus is generally reckoned as reigning from 106 or 104 B.C. to 79 B.C.—*Trans.*

[1] But adds in so many words: " Provided that you do nothing contrary to the commandments of the Church."—E. O.

and wills, so as not to be a despot abusing Omnipotence, to conquer, by suffering, the right to pardon rebellion. The woman has been audacious, she has desired to know; the man has been sublime, he has dared to love; and God, who while admiring strikes them, seems to have become jealous of the patience of his children.

All this is a revelation, poetic and esoteric; all this has occurred in the Human mind and in the Human heart. Man feels his high dignity when he wills to be free; the eternal vulture may tear the liver of Prometheus, but the courage of the great sufferer is reborn and grows ever with his daring. Jupiter avenges himself, but fears, and *he* will dethrone Jupiter and prove himself more a God than him, who will give his whole heart's blood to heal the wounds of Prometheus, and will come to suffer in his place.

Emancipation, Liberty, this is the final word of the Symbols. Jesus descended to Hell to kill the slavery of Death, and in re-ascending towards the light he dragged after him captivity, captive.

One day, Death alone will be dead; Curses alone will be accursed, and Damnation alone damned, and the Spirit of Light which desires that all men should be saved, all arrive at a knowledge of the truth, God —who after having made all human beings *en masse* responsible for the fault of a single one, may well pardon all on account of the merits of one—God will cause good to triumph, and evil will be destroyed.

The time will come when it will be realised that there is no true Liberty without Religion, no true

Religion without Liberty, but at present Religion and Liberty seem mutually to exclude and battle against each other. Like Religion, Liberty has her martyrs, and Liberty will deny authority so long as the Church denies the rights of Liberty.

"Ought we to concede to men the liberty of conscience?" asked our Doctors, and Rome decided in the negative, but that simply means that the Church does not renounce the direction of those who listen to her.

Liberty is not given, she is seized, or rather Nature gives her to us by the help of science; to ask whether one should allow to men, true men, the Liberty of conscience, is as if one asked whether we should allow them a head and a heart. Did not Galileo, even after he had withdrawn his learned demonstrations, know that the earth revolved? Will civilisation turn backwards, because there is a syllabus? Should the Pope forbid us to proceed? Let us salute the Pope and move on always. If the Holy Father wishes to make us hear him, he must e'en move on in his turn; it is full time for the shepherd to rise when his flock goes off. Hold! some one will say, your position as a Catholic does not permit you to speak thus.

If legitimate authority imposes silence on me I hold my tongue, *but* the earth revolves!

Conscience is inviolable, for it is divine, and it is in truth that which is essentially and absolutely free in man. For outside the conscience where can one find an absolute realisation of that ideal— Liberty?

From his cradle man is subjected to tyrannical necessities, and, like it or no, as he may, he must bear throughout his life that chain of obligations which society and nature emulate each other in imposing on him. Truth and Justice are austere mistresses, and Love is a despot, often cruel. For him who is not rich come the necessities of existence; there is no alternative between the yoke of labour and the work pillar [1] of misery. Those who are called the masters and the happy ones of the world have other enemies and other chains; so true is this that Alexander the Great almost envied the cynical half madness and indifference of Diogenes; but Diogenes and Alexander were the two extremes of paradoxical vanity; they were both the slaves of their Pride, and were not free men.

Liberty is the full enjoyment of all those rights which do not connote a duty. It is by the accomplishment of duty that rights are acquired and preserved. Man has the right to do his duty because he is bound to preserve his rights. Self-devotion is only a sublimation of duty, and it is the most sublime of all rights. A man may devote himself to another, but that is not being his slave; he may pawn his liberty, but he cannot alienate it without a species of moral suicide. A man may devote his life to the

---

[1] "*Ergastule.*" I never before met the word in French, but I take it to be derived from *ergastylos*, the pillar to which a recusant slave was chained to work; also the beams to which slaves in galleys were chained to row.—*Trans.*

triumph of an idea, but always reserving the right
of mental expansion and to a devotion to a worthier
object. *A perpetual vow is an affirmation of the
Absolute in the Relative, of Knowledge in Ignorance,
of the Immutable in the Transitory, of Contradiction
in all things.* It is, therefore, an engagement, null
and void, because it is rash and absurd and to repent
(and withdraw from it) when one realises its madness,
is not merely a right, but a duty.

It is true that the Church, whose decisions in
matters of Faith ought to be respected by all
Catholics, approves perpetual vows; but this is solely
when they are the result of a supernatural grace.'
Such vows are void before nature, but in the supernatural order they are sacred and inviolable.²

Marriage also is a perpetual engagement that
nature does not always ratify. Thence follow alike
the just but useless severities of morality and the
deterioration of manners. Thence follow in perpetual
contrast the tears and blood of the conjugal tragedy,
and the inexhaustible merriment of tales and comedy.
Moses is terrible when he descends from Mount Sinai
with horns; but why had he horns? Because he was
a married man,³ will perhaps reply some unblushing

' Or of a determined desire to obtain a supernatural
power. To command nature it is necessary to be
positive. She has no obedience for mixed mag-
netisms.—E. O.

² True.—E. O.

³ Behold a Frenchman! cynical and witty, even in
the midst of the arduous discussion of esoteric

Gaul, and because he had absented himself for forty nights from the conjugal couch! The old joke spares nothing.

The two greatest free-thinkers the world has known were Rabelais and Lafontaine, those two past Masters in wit and humour.[1] Both of them, moreover, good Catholics and free from any suspicion of heresy. Rabelais had taken religious vows and had the cleverness to make himself tolerated by the Pope. Lafontaine was married, and did not live with his wife; but what magicians of style! What apostles of the pure frank Truth! The work of Rabelais is the Bible of good sense and infallible gaiety; that of Lafontaine is the Evangel of Nature. Rabelais used to say mass, and if Lafontaine had lived in his time he doubtless would not have failed to assist in this by reading the prophecies of Baruch.

One ought to do what one likes, when one likes what one ought. This is the Law of Liberty! In other words, every man has the right to do his duty, but the first duty of man is set forth in the first commandment of the Decalogue.

---

philosophy. France has had several renowned Alchemists, she never had *one true Adept.*—E. O.

[1] It is impossible to translate adequately the original word "*gauloiserie*," with its double meaning and wide reaching significations. It is what Humpty Dumpty would have called a "portmanteau word" —*Trans.*

Thou shalt worship one God only, and him only shalt thou obey.[1]

And Jesus amplifying this precept, to the point of giving his explanation a paradoxical character, did not hesitate to add: You shall call no one in this world master or father; one only is your father, your master, and that is God.[2]

And St. John, the intimate confidant of the thoughts of Jesus, tells us that God is the Word, or Reason, " and the Word was God."

Therefore we have and we ought to have for master only Reason, or the Word which speaks.

For the Word, adds St. John, " was the true Light which lighteth every man that cometh into the world."

Jesus Christ said of himself: I am the principle that speaks.[3]

And every man who speaks in accordance with Reason can say, " I am Reason." And one ought to do and avoid what it prescribes, for the Will of Reason prevails over the Caprice of man. Caprice is the choice of amusements. One may pick and

---

[1] In the Massoretic Kabala, the *points* read: " One God, only—the TRUTH,—and her only shalt thou obey." Having so much of the Jesuit in him, E. L. could never become an adept.—E. O.

[2] God, or *Good*.—E. O.

[3] In this and many other cases, the *wording* of the authorised English version differs. But the sense is generally the same.—*Trans.*

choose where amusements are concerned, but not in the case of duty that imposes itself on us, and we are compelled to accept and do it.

Duty crushes him who seeks to avoid it, but bears onward with love him who accomplishes it.

To will what we ought, that is to will what God [1] wills. And when the will of man is the same as the divine will,[2] it becomes omnipotent.

Then it is that the miracles of Faith are accomplished ; then may we command the mountains to be moved, and the fruit trees to transplant themselves into the sea—words of our Saviour which are not to be taken in their literal sense.

The Word of Reason is efficacious, because it wills the end, and determines the means.

It is certain that neither the mountains nor the trees will remove themselves of their own accord.

The Force manipulates the Matter, and the Thought directs the Force.

Faith avails itself of Knowledge, and Knowledge directs Faith.

God himself can do nothing in opposition to Reason, which is the Law of Justice, because Justice, Law and Reason are God himself.

God does not arrest the sun and moon, to allow Joshua to slay certain Canaanites, and the announcement of such a miracle can only be a hyperbolical figure of speech of Oriental poetry.

[1] Or what Truth and Duty will.—E. O.
[2] Will—the Ākāsic Force.—E. O.

God does not reject a people after having chosen it, and he does not change his religion after having given it as eternal.

Arbitrary commands, favours, privileges, wrath, repudiation, pardon, belong only to the weakness of man.

But to make children gradually understand Reason, it is needful sometimes to throw over it an appearance of folly.

Childhood is naturally foolish; it must have its absurd stories and its sensational toys. It must have its automatic dolls, its animals moving by mechanism. It is true that it will very soon break these to see what is inside them.

And thus Humanity breaks one after the other all its childish Religions.

The true Religion is the eternal Religion.

The true Piety is the Piety that is independent. The true Faith is the absolute Faith which explains all Symbols and moves above all Dogmas. The true God is the God of Reason, and his true worship is Love and Liberty.

The Christians were right in breaking the idols, because men insisted on forcing *them* to adore these. The Protestants were right in trampling under foot, and burning the images of the Saints because, to compel them to worship these, men burnt the Protestants themselves.

Nevertheless what more Divine than the great works of Phidias and the Virgins of Raphael?

The worship of images, is it not the worship of Art, and was not the beautiful Religion of the Greeks one of the most graceful and splendid forms of the Universal Religion?

I adore truly the Divine Majesty before the Jupiter of Phidias, Immortal Beauty in the Venus of Milo, the Divinity of Man in the Christ of Michelangelo, the Dream of Heaven in the paradise of Fra Angelico.

But if to compel me to the worship of one or other of these, you show me scaffolds or blazing piles. . . . I would despise the executioner and turn my back on the idol!

Oh Madness of Human Tyranny!

In France, in the very country whose name even signifies Liberty, they raised scaffolds before the idol of Liberty herself.

Yet Robespierre and Marat cursed the Inquisitors as the Inquisitors had cursed Nero and Diocletian, and Marat and Robespierre have been cursed in their turn by later assassins, and Liberty still remains a gory Paradox, an Idol demanding sacrifices.

To this day the world has continued a great mad-house. Numbers have seized one, saying to him, "Worship my slipper, or I burn you!"

If the man who fell into their claws was cunning, he made believe to worship the slipper, and perhaps in so doing was neither a hypocrite nor an idolater,[1] but *their* victim is a guileless fellow, who takes the thing, in sad earnest, resists them, and becomes a Martyr!

The lassitude that succeeds to debauchery drives men to the madness of suicide, and the orgies of the

---

[1] Only a worthy son of Loyola!—E. O.

Decadence were bound to end fatally in the epidemic of Martyrdom. Young girls in those days skipped to the burning pile as to a dance ; infatuated mothers dragged their infants to the massacre. Executioners, tired of slaying, flung down their axes and begged for death. " Take off your neck-ruffs," wrote Tertullian to the Christian women, " and make room for the sabre of the executioners." Children played at Martyrdom, and one was seen red-heating fragments of iron to place upon his hand. The Roman cruelty provoked a reaction, and the taste for torture as an exhibition created a desire to experience it as a new sensation.

Polygnotus and Nearchus, interrupting a religious ceremony and overthrowing the altars of the Fatherland before a horrified people, do they seem to have acted as reasonable beings ? What then ? Did not St. Paul premise the folly of the cross ? And Jesus himself, did he not make a disturbance in the Temple of Jerusalem ? He was God, you will tell me. So be it, but humanly speaking his conduct was extremely irregular and very imprudent, and you would agree with me on this point . . . *if* you dared.

Is it lawful under the pretext that one is a God to be less prudent than a wise man ? This is what one has, if not the right, at least the inclination to inquire ; at least if one accepted the Gospels as history. But they are more than this ; they are precepts and symbols. God disapproves of commerce in Holy things ; he will not have traffic in his Temple, and the sellers deserve to be driven thence with blows of scourges; their shops should be overthrown; their money trampled under foot. This is all that the Legend (or if you will the Holy Evangel) of the sellers driven from the Temple signifies; here I bow and hold my peace.[1]

All is beautiful in our Religion when one knows how to understand it. All our Religion is true, and I would even dare to say that every Religion is true, apart from omissions, transpositions, wrong meanings, rash conjectures, additions, imaginings and misunderstandings.

This is what the free-thinkers must at last realise if they do not desire to be for ever battling against one of the most energetic forces of Human Nature, the invincible want to believe in, and adore something in the Infinite, and to have Faith in a Humanity greater in some respect than nature, so as to rise ever towards this, and to become purer in it, in order to conquer and to reign by it.

Voltaire did not desire to destroy Religion, but he wished to reduce it to a pure Deism. His motto was: "*God and Liberty*." He, who fancied himself a Poet, and yet understood nothing of the great Epic Poem of the Symbols, which starts from blind [2] Forces to

---

[1] Instead of canonising, the Church of Rome unfrocked and persecuted to his death poor Eliphas, the Abbé Louis Constant. "It is dangerous to leave things half undone," confessed the man when dying.—E. O.

[2] In the original, "*forces fatales*," by which I take it he means not merely "fatal forces," but the blind,

arrive at Intelligence and Liberty, stamps on suns, the sacred fire of Zoroaster, allows its robbery by Prometheus in defiance of the bolts of Jove, adores the force which it enchains at the feet of Beauty, traverses the splendid and almost infinite domain of glorious dreams, and finally accomplishes its synthesis in the reality of Man.

God is no longer the giant, invisible, fantastic. solitary, hidden in the unfathomable depths of Heaven, He is amongst us, he is in us, he has been born of the Woman, he is a babe whose new born cries we hear, a youth who thinks and loves, an outlaw who struggles and suffers, a free-thinker who protests, a reformer who drives out the buyers and sellers from the Holy Place, one accursed who blesses, and rises from the dead, the pure Man who pardons the adulterous Woman, the physician who heals, but also the sick man who hopes, the paralytic who arises and walks, the blind who opens his eyes. The others are me, said the Saviour, and he who sees me, sees also my Father; all that is done to the least of these is done to me, and God is in me, as I am in Him. Does He speak only of the chosen people of the blessed race of Abraham? No! for He blesses equally the good Samaritan, the Centurion, the woman of Canaan, and the immense herd of nations whom He hopes to gather into one fold. So he who gives bread to the poor,

---

unintelligent forces of the universe, that work on, slaves to the inherent laws of their being, and irresistible tyrants to all who have not pierced their secret.—*Trans.*

gives bread to God; he who consoles a sufferer,
consoles God; he who blesses an infidel, blesses God;
he who injures one man, injures God; he who curses
one man, curses God; he who slays one man, commits
Deicide.

What would Jesus have thought of the pitiless
Priest and Levite excommunicating and condemning
to death the good Samaritan as a schismatic, and the
wounded man of Jericho for having received with
gratitude the help and care of an infidel? What
must his judgment be on those Inquisitors who have
imprisoned, tortured, and burnt God alive? But the
God of these men was the Devil, and their Religion
was that of Anti-Christ. Man has no right to kill
man, except in self-defence.[1] The execution of a
criminal is a misfortune of war in a Society which is

---

[1] And not even then, for where would be the difference between the two?—E. O.

The difference would be that the one seeks to
kill, in violation of his neighbour's right to live,
aggressively, and not in defence of his own inherent right, whilst the other if he does also in-
fringe his neighbour's right to kill, does so only
defensively in vindication of his own inherent right to
live. There is a broad distinction between the two
cases that no sophistry can level; both *may* be wrong,
but even so (a moot point with the highest moralists
of all ages) there is a vast difference in the degree of
criminality in the two cases. E. O. condemns suicide
unconditionally, and rightly so, but to allow a man
to kill you, when you can prevent this by killing
him, is, it seems to me, suicide to all intents and
purposes.—*Trans.*

not yet Christian, but the executed one who accepts the expiation is the Father of the good thief dying on the cross with the Saviour, and we must see in him God severing himself from the brute. Crime is not a human act, but sacrifice is Divine when it is voluntary. *Homo sum humani a me nil alienum puto.* I am a man, and nothing human can be foreign to me. This is what God has said to the world in the Spirit of the Christian Revelation.

Let us seek God in Nature, let us worship Him in Spirit and in Truth, let us love and serve Him in Humanity. That is Religion, eternal and definitive.[2]

And when the chief of the Human Family have entered on this path, we shall be able to say with Voltaire: " God is Liberty," *for man will understand God, and will deserve to be free.*

Paradox III.—LOVE IS THE REALISATION

OF THE IMPOSSIBLE

LOVE is the Omnipotence of the Ideal. By the Ideal the soul is exalted ; it becomes greater than Nature, more living than the world, loftier than Science, more immortal than Life.

When Jesus Christ said: Love God with all your heart and your neighbour as yourself, this is the Law

---

' Only whatever we do let us call things by their right names, " *Pas de demi-inconnues.*"—E. O.

This is the end of this publication.

Any remaining blank pages are for our book binding
requirements and are blank on purpose.

To search thousands of interesting publications like this one,
please remember to visit our website at:

CPSIA information can be obtained at www.ICGtesting.com
Printed in the USA
LVOW03s1039300115

424975LV00020B/114/P

3208001